What is a . . . TRADEMARK?

Third Edition

ABA Section of Intellectual Property Law

Defending Liberty
Pursuing Justice

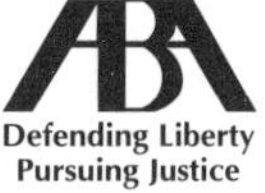

The American Bar Association would like to acknowledge the assistance of Professor Jay Erstling of the William Mitchell College of Law, and William Mitchell students Ashly Bew and Jason Melo in preparing the 2009 update of this publication.

Cover design by ABA Publishing.

12 11 10   5

What Is a Trademark?

Cataloging-in-Publication Data is on file with the Library of Congress
ISBN 13: 978-1-59031-770-9

Table of Contents

WHAT IS A TRADEMARK?

Two hundred years ago, trademark protection was the poorer cousin to the patent and copyright systems. While protection of an inventor's discovery or an author's writing was the subject of a constitutional mandate, protection of trademarks was left to the common law. There was reportedly little public interest in trademark protection.[1]

Today, trademarks may be protected under both state and federal statutes, as well as the common law. There are many marks for consumer products such as foods and beverages which are estimated to be worth tens or even hundreds of millions of dollars. Public interest in trademark protection is high and trademarks are often among a business's most valuable assets.

The Nature of a Trademark

What It Is

The Trademark Act of 1946, known as the Lanham Act, defines a trademark as follows:

> The term "trademark" includes any word, name, symbol or device or any combination thereof—
>
> (1) used by a person, or
> (2) which a person has a bona fide intention to use in commerce and applies to register on the principal register established by this Act,
>
> to identify and distinguish his or her goods, including a unique product, from those manufactured or sold by others and to indicate the source of the goods, even if that source is unknown.[2]

The statute provides a similar definition for "service marks," that is, marks which identify a service (e.g., banking, dry cleaning, restaurant) rather than goods. For convenience, it should be understood that as used hereafter, the terms "trademark" and "mark" include service marks. Although not found in the statute, the term "brand name" is sometimes used synonymously with "trademark."

---

[1] EDMUND W. KITCH & HARVEY S. PERLMAN, LEGAL REGULATION OF THE COMPETITIVE PROCESS (3d ed. 1986). *See also* FRANK I. SCHECTER, THE HISTORICAL FOUNDATIONS OF THE LAW RELATING TO TRADEMARKS (Col. Univ. Press 1925).
[2] 15 U.S.C. § 1127; Lanham Act § 45.

What It Does

A trademark has several functions. Arguably, the primary function is to identify the origin of the goods in connection with which the trademark is used. This is reflected in the statutory phrase "to identify and distinguish." It is not required that the purchaser know the identity of the source of goods as long as he or she recognizes that all goods bearing a particular trademark originate from a common, albeit anonymous, source. For example, while most people probably do not know that 9 LIVES cat food is made by Del Monte Corporation, they most likely do believe that all cat food labeled 9 LIVES comes from a single source.

Trademarks also provide quality assurance. For example, when a consumer dines at a MCDONALD'S or a WENDY'S restaurant, he or she expects that the nature and quality of the food served will be the same as that served at other restaurants bearing that name. A trademark induces the trademark owner to maintain a consistent level of quality, and allows consumers to rely on it.

What It Is Not

The term "trade name," according to modern usage, applies to names used to identify a business, such as a legal corporate name or an assumed name (or "dba").[3] Thus, trademarks are associated with goods while trade names identify businesses.

A Trademark Must Be Distinctive

Degree of Distinctiveness

A trademark must be distinctive, or recognizable as a mark, in order to serve its identification function. The degree of distinctiveness has important implications.

Marks are typically classified as (1) arbitrary or fanciful, (2) suggestive, (3) descriptive, or (4) generic.[4] An arbitrary or fanciful mark bears no relationship to the associated goods. It follows, therefore, that such a mark is inherently distinctive and readily distinguishes one merchant's goods from those of another. A "fanciful" mark is typically composed of coined words, while an "arbitrary" mark uses words that are in common use but bear no relationship to the associated goods. Fanciful marks include CLOROX,[5] KODAK[6] and

---

[3] 15 U.S.C. § 1127; Lanham Act § 45.
[4] The phrase "generic mark," although widely used, is an oxymoron; a generic term is really not a mark at all.
[5] Clorox Chem. Co. v. Chlorit Mfg. Corp., 25 F. Supp. 702 (E.D.N.Y. 1938).
[6] Eastman Kodak Co. v. Rakow, 739 F. Supp. 116 (W.D.N.Y. 1989).

POLAROID.[7] Arbitrary marks include APPLE for computers, and GREY GOOSE for vodka.

A "suggestive" mark suggests some quality or character of the associated goods, but not explicitly, so that some imagination is needed to determine the nature of the goods. Suggestive marks include JAGUAR for fast, luxurious cars and EXPLORER for an internet search engine. Suggestive marks, like arbitrary and fanciful marks, are inherently distinctive and readily registrable as trademarks.

In contrast, a "merely descriptive" mark identifies a characteristic, quality, purpose or some other aspect of a product or service. A descriptive mark is not inherently distinctive and is protectable or registrable only if it can be shown that consumers have learned to associate it with a single source. This learned association is called "acquired distinctiveness" or "secondary meaning." Marks found to be descriptive include CHAPSTICK[8] lip balm, RAISIN-BRAN[9] breakfast cereal and VISION CENTER[10] for a business offering optical goods and services. The statute provides that a showing of exclusive and continuous use of the mark in commerce by the applicant for five years is prima facie evidence of distinctiveness.[11]

A generic term is one that is used by the public to identify a category of goods, such as "beer," "shoes," or "automobile," to which a particular product belongs, e.g., MICHELOB, JOHNSTON & MURPHY or PORSCHE CARERRA. A generic term can never be a trademark. Examples of terms held to be generic include "lite beer"[12] for lower-calorie beer, "shredded wheat"[13] for cereal, and "super glue"[14] for a rapid-setting permanent adhesive.

A term which is generic for one product can be arbitrary when applied to another. For example, the word "trumpet" is generic for a type of musical instrument but would be arbitrary if used to designate an automobile. Furthermore, a term that is not initially generic may become so, if consumers come to believe that a mark is the generic name for a type of product. Marks that have become generic include "aspirin,"[15] "cellophane,"[16] and "escalator."[17]

---

[7] Polaroid Corp. v. Polaraid, Inc., 319 F.2d 830 (7th Cir. 1963).
[8] Morton Mfg. Corp. v. Delland Corp., 166 F.2d 191 (C.C.P.A. 1948).
[9] Skinner Mfg. Co. v. Kellogg Sales Co., 143 F.2d 895 (8th Cir. 1944).
[10] Vision Center v. Opticks, Inc., 596 F.2d 111 (5th Cir. 1979).
[11] 15 U.S.C. § 1052(f); Lanham Act § 2(f).
[12] Miller Brewing Co. v. G. Heileman Brewing Co., Inc., 561 F.2d 75 (7th Cir. 1977).
[13] Kellogg Co. v. Nat'l Biscuit Co., 305 U.S. 111 (1938).
[14] Loctite Corp. v. Nat'l Starch & Chem. Corp., 516 F. Supp. 190 (S.D.N.Y. 1981).
[15] Bayer Co. v. United Drug Co., 272 F. 505 (S.D.N.Y. 1921).
[16] DuPont Cellophane Co. v. Waxed Prod. Co., 85 F.2d 75 (2d Cir. 1936).
[17] Haughton Elev. Co. v. Seeberger, 85 U.S.P.Q. 80 (Comm'r Pats. 1950).

Appropriate Subject Matter for Trademarks

Virtually anything capable of indicating source may serve as a trademark. A few examples are discussed below.

Letters and numbers may be used as marks. For example, ABC, CBS and NBC are readily recognizable as the service marks of major radio and television broadcasting networks. Alphanumeric combinations such as V-8 vegetable juice and 7-ELEVEN convenience stores are also familiar marks.

Slogans can function as marks. For example, INTEL INSIDE indicates the source of microprocessor chips used in personal computers. Similarly, MAZDA used the slogan ZOOM-ZOOM as a trademark for its line of automobiles, and AMERICAN EXPRESS used DON'T LEAVE HOME WITHOUT IT for its credit card.

A color or combination of colors may function as an indicator of source and be registered as a trademark,[18] but only so long as there is a showing of secondary meaning. Musical notes, and other sounds, have been federally registered. The combination of notes "G, E and C," used by the National Broadcasting Company, were originally registered by the General Electric Company.[19] A federal registration has even been granted for a particular fragrance, reminiscent of plumeria, used to identify sewing thread.[20]

A product's "trade dress," which includes product features such as shape, texture, size, color and packaging, may also be protected if it is "nonfunctional." A feature is functional if it is necessary to a product's utility, or affects its cost and/or method of manufacture.[21] However, if other, different physical features can perform the same functions without sacrificing a functional advantage, the design may be considered non-functional.

Trademark Registration

The Benefits of Federal Registration

The law protects trademarks based on bona fide commercial use in commerce subject to Congressional regulation.[22] Registration does not create a trademark. Nonetheless, several very significant advantages are available to a trademark owner who registers a mark under federal law.

If a mark is inherently distinctive (arbitrary, fanciful or suggestive), or has become distinctive by having acquired secondary meaning, it can be registered

---

[18] Qualitex Co. v. Jacobson Products Co., 514 U.S. 159 (1995).
[19] *In re* General Electric Broadcasting Co., 199 U.S.P.Q. 560 (T.T.A.B. 1978).
[20] *In re* Clarke, 17 U.S.P.Q. 2d 1238 (T.T.A.B. 1990).
[21] Inwood Labs., Inc. v. Ives Labs, Inc., 456 U.S. 844 n.10 (1982).
[22] 15 U.S.C. § 1051; Lanham Act § 1.

on the Principal Register. A registration on the Principal Register is prima facie evidence of the validity of the mark,[23] the registrant's exclusive right to use the registered mark,[24] and the registrant's ownership of the mark.[25] A registration may become "incontestable" after five years on the Principal Register, if the appropriate affidavits are filed with the USPTO. Once a mark becomes incontestable, it becomes conclusive evidence of validity and ownership of the mark, and may only be canceled on certain limited grounds, such as genericness or fraud in obtaining the registration.[26]

These benefits are not afforded to marks registered on the Supplemental Register, which is reserved for descriptive marks that have not acquired secondary meaning.[27] However, registering the mark on the Supplemental Register provides notice to interested parties of the owner's claim to rights, may deter others from adopting and using the mark, will be cited by the Patent and Trademark Office as a basis for refusing to register confusingly similar marks, and provides a basis for registering the mark in many foreign countries.

How to Obtain a Federal Registration

An application for registration must be based on either use of or a bona fide intent to use the mark in commerce.[28] In order to demonstrate use in commerce the applicant must show that it has placed the mark on the goods (or on labels or tags affixed to the goods, packaging, or point of sale displays) and that the goods are sold or transported in interstate or foreign commerce. The "use in commerce" standard is liberal, but does not encompass token shipments made merely for purposes of reserving a mark or obtaining or maintaining a registration. In other words, the use must be "bona fide" commercial use.[29]

If an applicant has not used the mark in commerce, but has a bona fide intent to do so, it can file an intent-to-use ("ITU") application. A registration will not be granted, however, until the applicant files a verified statement that it has used the mark in commerce.

Trademark applications are examined by the United States Patent and Trademark Office ("PTO"). The application is assigned to an Examining Attorney who ensures that the application meets all statutory requirements and

---

[23] 15 U.S.C. §§ 1057(b), 1115(a); Lanham Act §§ 7(b), 33(a).
[24] *Id.*
[25] 15 U.S.C. § 1072; Lanham Act § 22.
[26] 15 U.S.C. §§ 1065, 1115(b); Lanham Act §§ 15, 33(b).
[27] 15 U.S.C. § 1094; Lanham Act § 26.
[28] A third basis exists as well, which concerns filing based on a foreign application or registration.
[29] 15 U.S.C. § 1127; Lanham Act § 45.

that the mark is registrable. Two of the most important determinations made by the Examining Attorney are whether the mark is distinctive as applied to the goods or services for which registration is sought, or whether the mark is confusingly similar to a mark that has already registered or is the subject of a prior application. If the mark appears to be registrable, the PTO will publish it for opposition in the *Official Gazette*. During the thirty-day period following publication, which can be extended for up to an additional 90 days without the applicant's consent, interested parties can oppose registration. If no one successfully opposes the application, the PTO will issue the registration if the application is use-based, or a Notice of Allowance for an ITU application.

After a Notice of Allowance is issued the applicant has six months, extendable in six-month increments for up to 30 additional months, to file a "statement of use," together with evidence of use. Assuming all requirements are met, the PTO then issues the Certificate of Registration.

International Registration Under the Madrid Protocol

International registration in certain countries is available through the Madrid system for the international registration of marks,[30] which is administered by the International Bureau of the World Intellectual Property Organization (WIPO).[31] The United States participates in the Madrid system as a member of the Madrid Protocol. The Madrid system allows a U.S. trademark owner to have its trademark protected in other member countries of the Madrid Protocol by filing a single application directly with the U.S. Patent and Trademark Office. A mark registered through the Madrid System must be based on one or more U.S. applications or registrations, and is equivalent to an application or registration filed directly in the countries designated in the International application. Guidance in the filing of International applications, including electronic forms for International applications, is available on the PTO web site.[32]

State Registration of Trademarks

Trademarks may be registered in every state, the District of Columbia and Commonwealth of Puerto Rico. In general, state registration provides few of the advantages of federal registration. However, issuance of a state registration may constitute evidence of ownership, and even validity of the mark in that

---

[30] 15 U.S.C. § 1141 *et seq.*
[31] *See* www.wipo.int/treaties/en/ip/madrid.
[32] www.uspto.gov.

jurisdiction. Most importantly, entering the mark on a state register provides notice of the owner's claim of rights to any parties who undertake a comprehensive trademark search.

Clearance Procedure

Before using a mark or filing for trademark registration, a party should check for possible conflicts with marks currently registered, in use, or for which applications have been filed. To check for conflicts, a search of state and federal trademark registrations, pending applications, business and trade directories, phone books, the internet and the like should be made. Some courts have found a lack of due diligence in failing to conduct a search to determine whether others might have prior rights to the mark.

How to Use a Trademark

A trademark or service mark may be identified by placing the designation™ or ^SM adjacent to it. These designations are used to identify unregistered trademarks, and indicate that trademark rights are claimed. Alternatively, an asterisk may be used instead of the ^TM designation, with an explanation that the mark is a trademark of a particular entity.

The statutory ® notice indicates that a mark is federally registered.[33] Other forms of statutory notice include the words "Registered in U.S. Patent and Trademark Office" or "Reg. U.S. Pat., & Tm. Off."[34] Using the statutory notice constitutes constructive notice of registration, and may preserve the right to collect damages for infringement of the mark without showing that the infringer had actual notice that the mark was a registered trademark. The ® symbol should not be used with marks that are not registered, or in countries where the mark is not registered.

When a mark appears in print or other textual media, it should be distinguished from the surrounding text by use of a different type size or style (e.g., ALL UPPER CASE or *italics*) and the appropriate notice (^®, ^TM or ^SM). The trademark should be used in conjunction with a generic term or descriptive word for the goods or services to emphasize the "brand" aspect of the mark. The mark should never be used as a noun. In fact, the word "brand" is often used with the mark to emphasize that the mark is a trademark, not the common name of a product. An example of this usage is " 'Post-it'® brand notes" for adhesive-backed paper pads sold by the 3M Company.

---

[33] 15 U.S.C. § 1111; Lanham Act § 29.
[34] *Id.*

A trademark must be used in order to maintain trademark rights. When use of a mark is discontinued with the intent not to resume use, the mark will be considered abandoned and unenforceable.[35] Failure to use a mark for three years will create a presumption that the mark has been abandoned.[36]

Trademarks as Property

Assignment

A trademark symbolizes—and derives its value from—the goodwill associated with the mark and the business associated with the mark. As a property right, a trademark exists only in connection with its associated product or service. A trademark cannot validly be transferred apart from the goodwill it symbolizes, and a valid assignment must contain an assignment of the goodwill associated with the mark.

In order to maintain rights in an acquired mark, the assigned trademark must be used on a product that is substantially similar to the product with which the trademark was used by the assignor. Accordingly, assignment of a mark may also require the transfer of any proprietary knowledge or equipment necessary to manufacture the product or offer the services sold under the mark.

Licensing

A trademark owner may license rights under the mark. A valid licensing arrangement requires that the licensor maintain control over the nature and quality of the goods sold under the mark. The quality assurance requirement protects the buying public by ensuring that consumers will get the quality of goods or services that they associate with the trademark. If a licensor fails to maintain the quality of the goods, loss of trademark rights can result. License provisions should include, at a minimum, acknowledgement of the licensor's right to control the nature and quality of the goods and right to inspect the licensee's operation, as well as the licensee's duty to provide samples of the goods bearing the mark upon the licensor's request.

Trademark Infringement

Infringement

Use of a mark that creates a likelihood of confusion among the relevant public as to the source of goods bearing the mark constitutes infringement.

---

[35] 15 U.S.C. § 1127; Lanham Act § 45.
[36] *Id.*

Confusion may arise through the use of a mark that is the same as or similar to an existing mark on or in connection with the same or similar goods or services. While an infringer's wrongful intent may be evidence of infringement and may also affect the amount of damages recoverable, wrongful intent is not required for a finding of infringement. The interest in protecting the public from confusion as to source is sufficient to trigger liability independent of an infringer's intent to deceive.

Likelihood of Confusion

In a trademark infringement action, the plaintiff must prove by a preponderance of the evidence (more likely than not) that defendant's use of the allegedly infringing mark will create a likelihood of confusion, mistake or deception in the minds of the relevant public as to the source of goods bearing the infringing mark, or as to sponsorship or approval of goods bearing the mark.[37]

A number of factors are analyzed in determining whether there is a likelihood of confusion, including the strength of the plaintiff's mark, the degree of similarity between the plaintiff's and the defendant's mark, the degree to which the plaintiff's and defendant's products or services are related, the likelihood that the plaintiff will expand its business into the same field of use as the defendant, the defendant's good faith in adopting its mark, evidence of actual confusion, the sophistication of the buyers, the cost of the products or services and the quality of the defendant's product. In any given case, some factors will weigh more heavily than others. Proof of bad faith can be decisive since one who has set out to deceive may be presumed to have succeeded, no matter how inept the attempt.

Counterfeiting

The Lanham Act distinguishes between a mark which is a "colorable imitation" of a registered mark and a "counterfeit" mark. The former is defined as a mark which "so resembles a registered mark as to be likely to cause confusion, mistake or to deceive."[38] A counterfeit mark, by contrast, is a "spurious mark which is identical with, or substantially indistinguishable from a registered mark."[39]

Goods associated with a counterfeit mark are typically imitations of an article associated with a well-known registered mark. The goods associated

---

[37] 15 U.S.C. § 1125(a)(1)(A); Lanham Act § 43(a)(1)(A).
[38] 15 U.S.C. § 1127; Lanham Act § 45.
[39] 15 U.S.C. § 1116(d); Lanham Act § 34(d).

with the counterfeit mark are usually priced significantly lower and are of lower quality than the genuine article. Under the Lanham Act, damages for infringement are ordinarily trebled if a party intentionally counterfeits a registered mark. Under the Customs Act, any articles imported into the U.S. bearing a counterfeit mark are subject to seizure and forfeiture.[40] Under the Trademark Counterfeiting Act of 1984, a person intentionally trafficking in goods or services who knowingly uses a counterfeit mark in connection with those goods or services may be fined up to $2,000,000 and imprisoned for up to ten years. An organization may be fined up to $5,000,000. For repeat offenders, the sanctions are even greater—up to $5,000,000 and 20 years imprisonment for an individual, and up to $15,000,000 for an entity.[41]

Dilution

The owner of a famous trademark may bring an action to stop another's use of a mark when the use is likely to cause dilution by tarnishment or dilution by blurring.[42] Dilution can occur regardless of whether the parties compete with each other or whether the other party's mark is likely to cause confusion.[43] Dilution by tarnishment occurs when an association arises from the similarity between the mark used and the famous mark that harms the reputation of the famous mark.[44] For example, the famous mark CANDYLAND for a children's game was diluted by tarnishment by the use of "candyland.com" for an Internet Web site containing sexually explicit material.[45]

A famous trademark is diluted by blurring when it is used by someone other than the owner and that use impairs the mark's distinctiveness,[46] meaning its ability to identify and distinguish the owner's goods or services. For example, the use of the mark VERIZON for clothing may cause the mark to become diluted by blurring. All relevant factors are considered when determining whether there is dilution by blurring, including the degree of similarity between the mark used and the famous mark, the degree of inherent or acquired distinctiveness of the famous mark, the extent to which the owner of the famous mark is engaging in substantially exclusive use of the mark, the degree of recognition of the famous mark, whether the user of the mark intended to create an associ-

---

[40] 19 C.F.R. § 133.21(b). Forfeiture occurs in the absence of written consent of the trademark owner.
[41] 18 U.S.C. § 2320(a).
[42] 15 U.S.C. § 1125(c)(1); Lanham Act § 43(c)(1).
[43] *Id.*
[44] 15 U.S.C. § 1125(c)(2)(C); Lanham Act § 43(c)(2)(C).
[45] Hasbro, Inc. v. Internet Entertainment Group, Ltd., 40 USPQ2d 1479 (W.D. Wash. 1996).
[46] 15 U.S.C. § 1125(c)(2)(B); Lanham Act § 43(c)(2)(B).

ation with the famous mark, and any actual association between the mark and the famous mark.[47]

An action for either type of dilution can be brought only if the trademark is famous, meaning it is widely recognized by the general consuming public of the United States as a designation of source of the goods or services of the mark's owner.[48] Fame is determined by evaluating all relevant factors, including the extent of actual recognition of the mark, the extent of sales of goods or services under the mark, the extent of advertising and publicity of the mark, and which party advertised/publicized the mark.[49]

Anticybersquatting Consumer Protection Act

The Anticybersquatting Consumer Protection Act (ACPA), established in 1999, prohibits the bad faith registration, trafficking in, or use of a domain name that is identical or confusingly similar to a distinctive trademark, including a personal name, or that dilutes a famous trademark.[50] The trademark owner may bring a civil action against the person liable; however, if a responsible defendant is not available, the trademark owner can bring an action against the domain name itself.[51]

To determine bad faith intent, a court generally considers factors such as: whether the domain name registrant has made bona fide prior use of the name, attempted to sell the name to the trademark owner without ever having used it, diverted consumers from the trademark owner's online location, provided misleading false contact information when applying for registration of the domain name, or registered multiple domain names that are identical or confusingly similar to distinctive marks.[52]

The ACPA defines "trafficking in" as "transactions that include, but are not limited to, sales, purchases, loans, pledges, licenses, exchanges of currency, and any other transaction for consideration or receipt in exchange for consideration."[53] For example, Virtual Works registered the domain name *vw.net* unaware that VW was a common abbreviation for VOLKSWAGEN automobiles. Virtual Works demonstrated bad faith under the ACPA when it offered to sell the domain name to Volkswagen.[54] In a similar case, the owner of the domain name

---

[47] *Id.*

[48] 15 U.S.C. § 1125(c)(2)(A); Lanham Act § 43(c)(2)(A).

[49] *Id.*

[50] 15 U.S.C. § 1125(d)(1)(A); Lanham Act § 43(d)(1)(A).

[51] 15 U.S.C. § 1125(d)(2)(A); Lanham Act § 43(d)(2)(A).

[52] 15 U.S.C. § 1125(d)(1)(B)(i); Lanham Act § 43(d)(1)(B)(i).

[53] 15 U.S.C. § 1125(d)(1)(E); Lanham Act § 43(d)(1)(E).

[54] Virtual Works, Inc. v. Volkswagen of America, Inc., 238 F.3d 264 (4th Cir. 2001).

fordworld.com, who had no relation to the Ford Motor Company, trafficked in the domain name in violation of the Act when he registered the domain name and offered to sell it to Ford.[55]

Remedies are offered to the owner of the mark but usually are limited to "a court order for the forfeiture or cancellation of the domain name or the transfer of the domain name to the owner of the mark."[56] Volkswagen was granted the right to use *vw.net* for itself, for example, because Virtual Works tried to profit in bad faith from Volkswagen's mark.[57]

---

[55] Ford Motor Company v. Peter Catalanotte, 342 F.3d 543 (6th Cir. 2003).
[56] 15 U.S.C. § 1125(d)(1)(D)(i); Lanham Act § 43(d)(1)(D)(i).
[57] Virtual Works, Inc. v. Volkswagen of America, Inc., 238 F.3d 264 (4th Cir. 2001).

About the ABA Section of Intellectual Property Law

From its strength within the American Bar Association, the ABA Section of Intellectual Property Law (ABA-IPL) advances the development and improvement of intellectual property laws and their fair and just administration. The Section furthers the goals of its members by sharing knowledge and balanced insight on the full spectrum of intellectual property law and practice, including patents, trademarks, copyright, industrial design, literary and artistic works, scientific works, and innovation. Providing a forum for rich perspectives and reasoned commentary, ABA-IPL serves as the ABA voice of intellectual property law within the profession, before policy makers, and with the public.